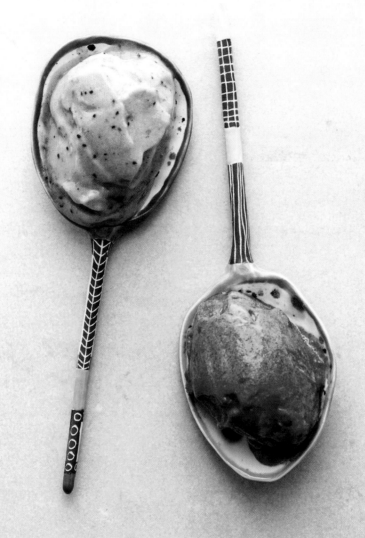

PØRRIDGE

PØRRIDGE

OATS + SEEDS + GRAINS + RICE

ANNI KRAVI

quadrille

Publishing Director: Sarah Lavelle

Creative Director: Helen Lewis

Junior Commissioning Editor: Romilly Morgan

Senior Designer: Nicola Ellis

Photographer: Andrew Taylor

Food and Prop Stylist: Anni Kravi

Food Coordinator: Richard McCormick

Production: Vincent Smith and Tom Moore

First published in 2017 by
Quadrille Publishing
Pentagon House
52-54 Southwark Street
London SE1 1UN
www.quadrille.co.uk
www.quadrille.com

Quadrille is an imprint of Hardie Grant
www.hardiegrant.com.au

Reprinted in 2017
10 9 8 7 6 5 4 3 2

Cataloguing in Publication Data: a catalogue record for
this book is available from the British Library.

ISBN: 978 1 84949 903 3

Printed in China

CONTENTS

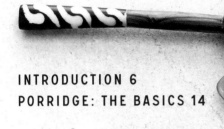

INTRODUCTION

DON'T THINK OF PORRIDGE AS JUST YOUR REGULAR MORNING BOWL OF OATS, AS IT IS SO MUCH MORE...

...Instead think of cooked porridge, baked porridge, raw porridge, savoury porridge, porridge snack bars, porridge with rye, porridge with spelt, rice porridge, buckwheat and amaranth porridge. In this book, there are recipes for breakfast, lunch, dinner, snacks and dessert. This humble bowl of grains and milk can be turned into a complete meal with the right toppings – berries, nuts, seeds, coconut and even edible flowers – arranged beautifully on top.

In PØRRIDGE, I've created recipes for both sweet and savoury porridges, cooked and uncooked versions, made with not only oats but also many other whole grains, such as spelt, quinoa and buckwheat. Additionally, I've included smoothie bowls, snacks and, of course, toppings, as no porridge base would be complete without its toppings and there are also recipes for making your own cooking and soaking liquids, such as plant milks and yogurts.

I have always been a lover of porridge [as most Finnish people are]: oatmeal porridge, rye porridge, Christmas porridge, semolina porridge and whipped berry porridge *vispipuuro* to name just a few, traditional Finnish favourites of mine. However, although I have cooked porridge all my life, it was only when I visited a porridge-only restaurant while travelling, that I started thinking about porridge as something savoury as well as sweet. This is when I began experimenting with various grains and milks and started to include different spices and all kinds of ingredients into my humble bowls.

BASES

It all starts with a good base. I prefer using milk to water and plant milk to dairy milk when cooking my porridge bowls. As an alternative, I buy organic unsweetened oat, soy or coconut milk and try to have a batch of homemade nut or seed milk in my fridge. Homemade nut milk is not only delicious and quite easy to make, but it's also cheaper than most good-quality shop-bought nut milks. Moreover, you can play around with different flavour options and adjust the sweetness to your taste. The same applies to plant yogurt alternatives.

SWEET COOKED PORRIDGE

Imagine a Finnish winter. It's freezing cold and dark from 2p.m. until 10a.m. Would you not crave something super-comforting for breakfast, like a hearty bowl of cooked porridge? I am a seasonal eater and these sweet, cooked porridges are my go-to breakfast for any chilly day. I love adding banana to my porridge bases, as it gives them a creamy and thick texture as well as a healthy quantity of natural sweetness. Most of my cooked recipes use bananas as they contain a good amount of energy and are packed with fibre, potassium and vitamins which help the brain produce serotonin, the neurotransmitter that makes you feel happy [even when it's cold and dark outside]. However, if you don't like bananas, there are also banana-free versions, using other fruit and vegetables like apples and carrots.

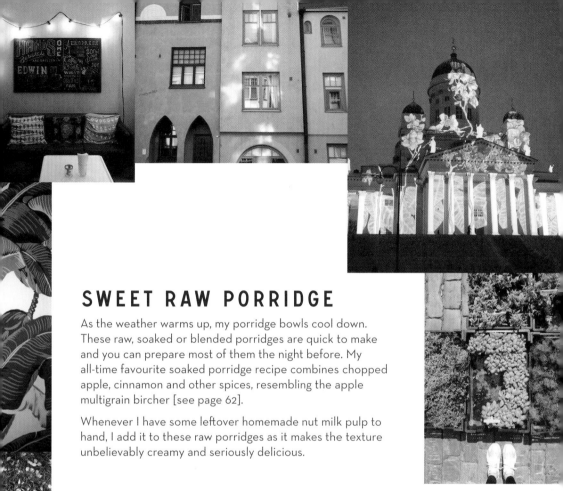

SWEET RAW PORRIDGE

As the weather warms up, my porridge bowls cool down. These raw, soaked or blended porridges are quick to make and you can prepare most of them the night before. My all-time favourite soaked porridge recipe combines chopped apple, cinnamon and other spices, resembling the apple multigrain bircher [see page 62].

Whenever I have some leftover homemade nut milk pulp to hand, I add it to these raw porridges as it makes the texture unbelievably creamy and seriously delicious.

SAVOURY PORRIDGE

These porridges are akin to risottos. Easy and quick to cook, all these bowls make a nourishing meal, and can be packed into a container and taken to work. The base can be anything from basic oats to buckwheat, amaranth, quinoa or rice. By adjusting the amount of liquid used in the cooking, almost anything can be turned into a porridge. I love adding some starchy vegetables like sweet potato or beetroot for a hint of sweetness and a hot pink colour to the porridge. Add some chia 'eggs' [see page 33], beans or tofu for protein, then throw in a rainbow of veggies and you suddenly have a delicious and completely balanced meal.

MY FOOD PHILOSOPHY

After dealing with lots of stress-related stomach issues, food intolerances and sleeping problems I started my website blueberryboost.com and Instagram @anniskk to document my journey towards better health, happiness and well-being. This project has helped me to find a balanced healthy, wholesome diet. I believe that when you stick to home cooking with real ingredients most of the time, you can eat out at weekends without losing track of those healthy habits that make the most of your overall well-being. What works best for me is a whole food, plant-based diet consisting of a huge variety of vegetables, whole grains, pulses, nuts, seeds and added boosts from certain 'superfoods'. This is my understanding of balance.

ABOUT ANNI

I graduated from Aalto University School of Business in 2015 with a Masters in economics and business administration. After working part time as a freelance foodie and digital content creator, recipe writer and food stylist I made nutritious food my main focus and co-founded DATE + KALE, a healthy, plant-based food concept in Helsinki.

You will notice that the recipes in this book are plant-based, refined sugar- and dairy-free and most of the recipes are also gluten-free. However, I don't follow a specific food philosophy or label myself as vegan, raw foodist or gluten-free. Instead, I just eat simple, wholesome food from fresh ingredients, always seasonal and organic when possible and food that makes me feel good.

*If you are vegan, some recipes in this book contain bee pollen or honey, so do substitute with a suitable vegan sweetener such as coconut nectar or maple syrup.

MINDFULNESS

As well as creating, sharing and learning about new ways of cooking, eating raw food and preparing wholesome meals, blueberryboost has been [and still is] my journey to combine food with my other two passions: art and photography. It's not only how the food tastes and what it is made of but also how it looks. Beautifully presented, lovingly prepared food feeds your soul much more than a messy plateful of veggies and grains. I find cooking meditative and it's my way of relaxing, clearing my mind and letting go of the daily distractions in life. Some people meditate in the morning, but you will find me preparing a breakfast bowl mandala with the same intention and focus. I find this mindfulness practice makes a huge difference to my day.

Of course, we don't always have as much time to prepare our meals as we would like to. But when we do have a little more time, I encourage you to use the opportunity to create beautiful dishes. Challenge yourself, be creative and don't worry if it doesn't turn out perfect.

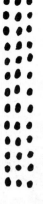

PORRIDGE:
THE BASICS

I make my own plant milks on a weekly/bi-weekly basis, but I also buy ready-made coconut, soy or oat milk. These have a much longer shelf life than raw, fresh nut milk [which usually keeps fresh for just 2–3 days in the fridge]. For plant-based yogurt alternatives, I like shop-bought unsweetened soy or oat 'gurt' whenever I don't have my homemade, delicious nut 'rawgurt' [see page 36] to hand.

For sweetening and seasoning, I use unrefined, organic varieties of both sugar and salt. I prefer fresh fruit such as bananas or dates for sweetening. If you feel that some of my recipes need a little extra sweetness, then do add more coconut nectar, maple syrup or raw honey. When it comes to seasoning, Himalayan salt and tamari soy sauce are my favourites and it's also worth experimenting with the addition of dried nori seaweed instead of salt for a lower sodium option. On top of my savoury porridges, I add a splash of coconut or sesame oil [for healthy fats] as well as freshly squeezed lemon, raw apple cider vinegar or brown rice vinegar for acidity. For sweet bowls, I like to add flax, chia or hemp seeds as well as raw, unsweetened nut or seed butters.

In addition to these staple items, I stock up on seasonal fresh produce each week: leafy greens, root vegetables, herbs, fruit and berries. In general, I prefer local berries to fruit or imported 'exotic' berries: wild blueberries or bilberries, blackcurrants, sea buckthorn berries and cloudberries are my absolute favourites. All these berries are true Nordic 'superfoods' as they contain a wide range of vitamins and antioxidants and sea buckthorn berry oil is widely regarded in Finland as a beautifying ingredient. Apples, spinach, strawberries and citrus fruit are my top four organic staples as they contain the most pesticide residues from non-organic farming.

Finally, for home cooking I usually choose just plant-based protein alternatives like tofu and tempeh as well as a variety of complete proteins [containing all the essential amino acids] such as legumes – edamame beans, chickpeas and black beans. If you want to substitute some of the plant proteins in these recipes for some sustainable seafood, or use organic free-range [cage-free] eggs instead of chia 'eggs' or swap plant yogurt for organic dairy yogurt, then go for it. Do what feels right for you.

WHAT'S IN MY KITCHEN?

GRAINS [ORGANIC]

OATS [WHOLEGRAIN]: Naturally gluten-free [but check the label for a 100% gluten-free variety]. These are mild tasting and a good source of fibre and betaglucane. Oats also create the creamiest bowl of porridge.

RYE [WHOLEGRAIN]: A dark, strong tasting and high-fibre grain that Scandis love.

SPELT [WHOLEGRAIN]: An ancient, high-fibre grain relative of wheat but easier to digest and lower in gluten. It is great for porridge and muesli as well as bread and pancakes and has a nutty flavour.

RICE [BROWN + BLACK VARIETIES]: Gluten-free with a nutty flavour, the black variety is very high in antioxidants. It is my favourite grain for savoury porridge.

SEEDS + NUTS [ORGANIC]

QUINOA [SEEDS + FLAKES]: A gluten-free and high-protein grain. Quinoa flakes and seeds are great for porridge paired with some raw cacao powder. The seeds require longer cooking time and need to be rinsed before use.

AMARANTH [SEEDS]: These are gluten-free and high in protein, similar to quinoa but with an even smaller grain. Amaranth seeds tend to turn sticky when cooked so they make great porridge [especially savoury]. Rinse amaranth before cooking.

BUCKWHEAT [RAW GROATS]: Gluten-free with a mild, earthy taste, these are my favourite grains for raw porridge, but they also work well in the cooked versions. Rinse buckwheat groats multiple times before use to prevent stickiness. For raw porridge, rinse buckwheat at least three times, then soak overnight and rinse again in the morning.

CHIA SEEDS: High in protein and fibre, chia seeds can be used to make puddings and jams. When soaked they can be used to make a plant-based egg substitute. These seeds are good for the stomach and packed with healthy Omegas.

HEMP HEARTS: Packed with protein, vitamins and minerals, I love the shelled variety for sprinkling on top of smoothie bowls or making plant milk.

FLAXSEEDS [GROUND + WHOLE]: High in fibre and Omegas, these seeds can be used instead of eggs to give texture to your bowls.

TAHINI [LIGHT, DARK, UNSALTED + SALTED]: A sesame seed spread that comes in light, brown and black varieties. It is high in calcium and minerals. Drizzle tahini on top of sweet or savoury porridges.

PEANUT BUTTER [UNSALTED, SMOOTH + FREE OF PALM FAT]: High in protein and energy and work best with apples or carrots.

ALMOND BUTTER [UNSALTED]: High in healthy fats with a relatively mild flavour, this is my favourite nut butter to add on top of any sweet porridge.

PUMPKIN SEED BUTTER [UNSALTED]: A high protein and strong tasting spread to add on top of sweet porridges.

PRODUCE [ORGANIC]

LEAFY GREENS: Kale, spinach and seasonal dark greens all contain lots of vitamins, minerals and chlorophyll.

VEGETABLES: Carrots, sweet potato, beetroot, butternut squash, broccoli and cauliflower.

HERBS: Coriander, basil, flat-leaf parsley and Thai basil all add a deeper flavour to your dishes.

EDIBLE FLOWERS: Violets are my daily morning magic.

FRUIT: Bananas, apples, dates, lemons and limes add a natural sweetness and acidity. I love using the rind from [organic] citrus fruits for extra flavour and sometimes I even blend the whole fruit in a high-speed blender.

BERRIES: I recommend using fresh, wild blueberries, strawberries, raspberries, sea buckthorn berries, black- and redcurrants, cranberries, lingonberries and cloudberries as they all contain lots of vitamins and antioxidants but I have given alternatives which are commonly available worldwide.

MEDJOOL DATES: It's worth noting that I always prefer using this variety of dates in my recipes. In my opinion, Medjool dates are the most delicious variety on the market.

PLANT MILKS [ORGANIC]

HEMP [HOMEMADE]: A high protein 'instant milk' as the seeds don't need to be soaked and the milk doesn't need to be drained.

CASHEW [HOMEMADE]: This is a light, creamy milk that I usually spice with cinnamon. It brings richness to any porridge and can be heated gently. Use the pulp for an extra creamy porridge texture.

ALMOND [HOMEMADE]: This milk is great in chia pudding and in raw and cooked porridges. Almond milk can separate a bit when heated, so it's better to add at the end of cooking. Use the pulp for an extra creamy raw porridge texture.

OAT [SHOP-BOUGHT, UNSWEETENED]: This milk withstands heat well and works with any porridge recipe. It has a mild flavour and is the easiest plant milk to buy.

COCONUT [SHOP-BOUGHT, FULL-FAT]: My favourite base for cooking Asian-style porridges, especially rice-based savoury porridges.

SEASONING + SWEETENING

HIMALAYAN SALT: This is pink, unrefined salt with trace minerals that I recommend using for all my recipes.

TAMARI SOY SAUCE: My favourite seasoning for tofu, tempeh or kale.

BROWN RICE VINEGAR: A mild vinegar for seasoning Asian dishes and especially rice-based porridge. It can also be used as a pickling vinegar.

UMEBOSHI VINEGAR: My favourite vinegar for seasoning kale or other greens, it is made from Japanese umeboshi plums.

RAW APPLE CIDER VINEGAR: This is my favourite 'standard' vinegar for everything!.

COCONUT OIL [VIRGIN, RAW]: This oil can stand high heat so it is ideal for frying. I like adding a spoonful to my savoury porridge.

COCONUT BUTTER OR MANNA: This is made from dried coconut flesh. I eat it straight out of the jar or add a spoonful to my porridge base or spread it on top of snack bars.

COCONUT NECTAR [LIGHT]: My favourite unrefined sweetener, as it has a mild flavour and it's not too sweet.

UNREFINED SESAME OIL [LIGHT, NOT TOASTED]: Great frying oil for tofu or tempeh, look for a variety that is not toasted as it has a much milder flavour. I recommend using the unrefined variety for all my recipes.

OLIVE OIL [EXTRA-VIRGIN]: This oil works best raw or lightly heated.

HONEY [RAW MANUKA HONEY]: This is known for its anti-inflammatory benefits. It works well with cinnamon and turmeric.

MAPLE SYRUP: A less refined sweetener if you feel that a recipe needs some extra sweetness; my favourite combination is maple syrup with carrot.

BEANS + PROTEIN [ORGANIC]

TOFU [EXTRA FIRM, NAKED]: A plant-based complete protein made from soya beans. Choose organic and non-genetically modified [GMO] whenever possible. It is pretty flavourless when it isn't marinated but tastes great seasoned with some sesame oil, miso paste or tamari. Raw or lightly cooked is best.

TEMPEH [NAKED OR SMOKED]: A plant-based and fermented complete protein made from soya beans or broad beans, peas or buckwheat. Choose organic and non-GMO whenever possible. Buy smoked tempeh or season yourself with some tamari and spices.

EDAMAME BEANS [ORGANIC, NON-GMO]: These are green, young soya beans [my favourite beans] and a complete protein. Choose organic and non-GMO whenever possible.

CHICKPEAS: A complete source of protein and makes perfect hummus or savoury porridge topping.

BLACK BEANS: These are a complete source of protein with a creamy flavour. They work especially well in Mexican-inspired dishes.

WHERE TO FIND INGREDIENTS

Most of the ingredients in this book are readily available from good-quality health food stores. For the harder to find ingredients, I recommend that you look at online shops, such as: amazon.com, wholefoodsmarket.com and hollandandbarrett.com as they often have more budget friendly alternatives.

When I am travelling, I love searching for and discovering new brands and ingredients. Whenever I find something new, I usually take it back home to try out in my kitchen. It's almost like I am taking a part of that trip back home so I can rediscover it again in Helsinki.

EQUIPMENT

HIGH-SPEED BLENDER: I use a Vitamix for blending smoothie bowls, raw porridges, nut milks, butters, bliss balls and desserts. I also use a high-speed blender for blending any spreads or sauces in large quantities. However, you can use a less powerful blender for blending smoothie bowls and raw porridges.

STICK BLENDER: I use a stick blender for blending banana 'ice cream', hummus, pesto, cashew 'cheeze' and hemp heart 'parmesan' as I find it easier to use when blending smaller quantities. However, if you are making larger batches, a high-speed blender is more time efficient.

JUICER: I use a juicer to extract fruit and vegetable juice. When juicing fruits or vegetables, almost all the insoluble fibre from the plants gets extracted and comes out as the pulp – you can save the vegetable pulp to make pesto and hummus or fruit juice pulp to blend into smoothie bowls or use as a porridge or yogurt topping. [Make sure that you use the pulp immediately.]

NUT MILK BAG: For making creamy, smooth homemade nut milk you will need either a nut milk bag or a thin, muslin [cheesecloth] fabric to strain the liquid through.

GLASS JARS: I store my nut milks, nut butters, spreads, sauces and overnight porridges in airtight sterilized glass jars. Make sure you sterilize the jars before using.

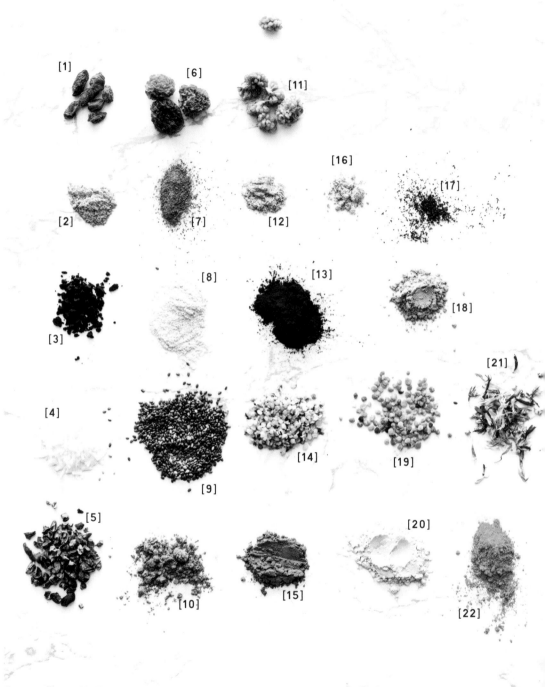

MY SUPERPOWDERS
+ SPRINKLES

[1] goji berries

[2] ginger

[3] reishi mushroom

[4] desiccated coconut

[5] cacao nibs

[6] inca berries

[7] cinnamon

[8] ashwagandha

[9] black chia seeds

[10] carob

[11] white mulberries

[12] cardamom

[13] spirulina

[14] hemp hearts

[15] raw cacao

[16] nutmeg

[17] bourbon vanilla

[18] wheatgrass

[19] bee pollen

[20] maca

[21] dried cornflower sprinkle

[22] turmeric

[23] sea buckthorn berry powder

[24] freeze-dried blackcurrant
     powder

[25] freeze-dried
     lingonberry powder

[26] freeze-dried wild
     blueberry powder

BASES

ALMOND MILK

110g [1 cup]	raw almonds
2	dates, pitted
pinch	salt

MAKES ABOUT 1 LITRE [4½ CUPS]

Soak the almonds in a bowl of water overnight, then drain and rinse thoroughly.

Put the almonds in a high-speed blender with 750ml [3 cups] water and blend for about 1–2 minutes. Add the dates and salt, then blend again for another 1–2 minutes. Pour the nut milk through a nut milk bag or cheese strainer into a bowl. Squeeze or 'milk' the bag so that all the liquid comes through and the pulp is left in the bag. Repeat until you have gathered all the liquid.

Store in sterilized bottles or jars for 2–3 days in the fridge.

TIP: Save the pulp for blending into raw porridges to add an extra creamy texture.

VANILLA
HEMP MILK

100g [1 cup]	shelled hemp seeds
3	dates, pitted
1 tsp	vanilla powder

MAKES ABOUT 1 LITRE [4 $\frac{1}{2}$ CUPS]

Blend all the ingredients together in a high-speed blender with 900ml [3 $\frac{3}{4}$ cups] water. Pour into a sterilized airtight glass jar, cover with a lid and store in the fridge for 2–3 days.

CINNAMON CASHEW MILK

110g [1 cup]	cashews
1 tsp	ground cinnamon
pinch	salt
1–2 tsp	coconut nectar, to taste

MAKES ABOUT 1 LITRE [4½ CUPS]

Soak the cashews in a bowl of water for at least 4 hours, then rinse thoroughly and drain.

Put the cashews and 750ml [3 cups] water in a high-speed blender and blend for about 1–2 minutes. Add the remaining ingredients and blend again for another 1–2 minutes. Pour the nut milk through a nut milk bag or cheese strainer into a bowl. Squeeze or 'milk' the bag so that all the liquid comes through and the pulp is left in the bag. Repeat until you have gathered all the liquid.

Store in sterilized bottles or jars in the fridge for 2–3 days.

TIP: Save the pulp for blending into raw porridges to add an extra creamy texture.

CHIA
'EGGS'

2 tbsp	chia seeds or ground flaxseeds

MAKES 2 'EGGS'

Mix the seeds and 6 tbsp water together in a small bowl. Leave to stand for 10–15 minutes until it is a thick, egg-like consistency.

POMEGRANATE + LEMON JUICE

2	pomegranates
$\frac{1}{2}$	lemon
	ice cubes
5	fresh mint leaves

MAKES 1 LARGE OR 2 SMALL GLASSES

Cut the pomegranates in half and remove the seeds. The simplest way to do this is to place the pomegranate half on the top of your palm, skin-side up, and using a spoon, gently knock the skin so that the seeds start falling out.

Wash the lemon half in hot water, then cut it into cubes [choose organic lemons with a thin skin to avoid bitterness]. Put the pomegranate seeds and lemon cubes into a juicer and juice it all up! Pour into glasses and serve with ice cubes and some fresh mint leaves.

NUT 'RAWGURT'

35g [$\frac{1}{4}$ cup]	cashews
55g [$\frac{1}{2}$ cup]	raw almonds
$\frac{1}{2}$ tsp	vanilla powder
2	dates, pitted
3 tbsp	ground flaxseeds

SERVES 4-6

Soak the cashews and almonds in a bowl of water overnight, then drain and rinse thoroughly.

Put the almonds, cashews, 400ml [$1\frac{2}{3}$ cups] water, vanilla and dates into a blender and whizz until smooth. Pour the 'rawgurt' into a sterilized glass jar, mix in the ground flaxseeds until combined, then chill in the fridge to thicken and cool for 1–2 hours.

Decorate with toppings of your choice.

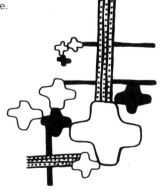

TIP: If you haven't eaten bee pollen before, start with a small dose and increase it gradually, to ensure you can tolerate it.

SWEET

COOKED PORRIDGE

RAW PORRIDGE

SMOOTHIE BOWLS

TURMERIC, CACAO + BUCKWHEAT

200ml [scant 1 cup]	oat milk
70g [½ cup]	raw buckwheat groats, well rinsed
1 tsp	raw cacao powder
½ tsp	ground turmeric
1	large, fresh banana, mashed
pinch	salt

+ TOPPINGS

2 tbsp	blackcurrant + vanilla chia 'jam' [see page 134]
1 tbsp	fresh lingonberries or cranberries
1 tbsp	fresh cloudberries or raspberries
1 tsp	cacao nibs
1 tsp	desiccated coconut

MAKES 1 BOWL

Heat 100ml [7 tbsp] water and 100ml [7 tbsp] of the oat milk in a small saucepan and bring to the boil. Add the buckwheat with the cacao and turmeric, then reduce the heat to low and cook for 10 minutes, or until almost all the liquid has been absorbed. Add the banana, the remaining oat milk and the salt, then cook for a further 5 minutes until the banana has combined into the mixture.

Serve the porridge with the 'jam', berries, cacao nibs and coconut.

SIMPLE
THREE-GRAIN

200ml [scant 1 cup]	oat milk
1 tbsp	rolled oats
1 tbsp	rye flakes
1 tbsp	spelt flakes
$\frac{1}{2}$ tsp	vanilla powder
1 tbsp	ground flaxseeds
1	large, fresh banana, mashed
pinch	salt

+   TOPPINGS

1 tbsp	fresh blueberries or bilberries
2 tbsp	fresh raspberries
2 tbsp	homemade date 'chutney' [see page 133]
1 tsp	black tahini [see page 138]
1 tsp	bee pollen [optional]
1 tsp	dried flower sprinkle [optional]

MAKES 1 BOWL

Heat 100ml [7 tbsp] water and 100ml [7 tbsp] of the oat milk in a small saucepan until it is almost boiling.

Meanwhile, mix the grains, vanilla and flaxseeds together in a small bowl, then add this to the milk. Stir, reduce the heat to low and cook for 2–3 minutes until the porridge starts to thicken. Add the banana, then add the remaining oat milk. Stir and cook for a further 2–3 minutes until the banana has combined into the mixture. Add the salt and stir once more. Remove from the heat, cover with a lid and leave to stand for a couple of minutes.

Pour the porridge into a serving bowl and top with blueberries, raspberries, date 'chutney' and tahini. Sprinkle with bee pollen and dried flowers, if using.

SPICED
COCONUT MILK
+ BROWN RICE

70g [⅓ cup]	brown rice
½ tsp	ground cinnamon
½ tsp	ground cardamom
½ tsp	ground turmeric
pinch	salt
200ml [scant 1 cup]	full-fat coconut milk

 TOPPINGS

2 tbsp	pomegranate seeds
1 tbsp	liquorice almonds [see page 130]
1 tbsp	homemade date 'chutney' [see page 133]
sprinkle	ground cinnamon

MAKES 1 BOWL

Put the brown rice, spices, salt and 100ml [7 tbsp]
water into a small saucepan and cook over a
medium heat until all the water has been absorbed.
Add the coconut milk and 150ml [10 tbsp] water,
then reduce the heat to low, cover and cook for
40–45 minutes, stirring occasionally and making
sure the rice doesn't burn or stick on the base
of the pan. When the porridge consistency is to
your liking, pour it into a serving bowl and serve
with pomegranate seeds, liquorice almonds, date
'chutney' and a sprinkle of ground cinnamon.

This recipe is my spiced version of a traditional rice porridge we cook during Christmas time in Finland. I am using brown rice instead of white as it contains extra fibre, and coconut milk instead of cow's milk as a dairy-free option.

BAKED
BLUEBERRY
BANANA BREAD

35g [scant ½ cup]	rolled oats
1 tbsp	ground flaxseeds
½ tsp	ground cardamom
70g [½ cup]	fresh blueberries or bilberries
1	large, fresh banana
100ml [7 tbsp]	oat milk
pinch	salt

TOPPINGS

1 tbsp	fresh blueberries
1 tbsp	fresh cloudberries or raspberries
1 tbsp	fresh raspberries
1 tbsp	dried mulberries
½ tbsp	nut butter of choice
1 tsp	dried flower sprinkle [optional]

MAKES 1 BOWL

Preheat the oven to 180°C/350°F/Gas 4.

In a small bowl, mix the oats, flaxseeds, cardamom and salt together.

Blend the blueberries, banana and oat milk together in a high-speed blender until smooth, then mix into the oats to combine.

Pour the mixture into an ovenproof bowl or dish and bake in the oven for about 20 minutes.

Top with the fresh and dried berries, a spoonful of nut butter and a sprinkle of dried flowers, if using.

CARROT, HONEY + RYE

200ml [scant 1 cup]	vanilla hemp milk [see page 28]
1 tbsp	rye flakes
20g [$\frac{1}{4}$ cup]	rolled oats
1 tbsp	chia seeds
$\frac{1}{2}$ tsp	ground cinnamon
$\frac{1}{2}$ tsp	honey, or maple syrup for a vegan option
2	small carrots, peeled and grated
pinch	salt

+ TOPPINGS

1 tbsp	fresh raspberries
1 tbsp	fresh blackcurrants
1 tbsp	fresh sea buckthorn berries or cranberries
1 tbsp	dried inca berries
1 tbsp	coconut flakes
1 tsp	bee pollen [optional]

MAKES 1 BOWL

Bring 100ml [7 tbsp] of the vanilla hemp milk and 100ml [7 tbsp] water to the boil in a small saucepan.

Mix the rye, oats, chia seeds and cinnamon together in a bowl, then add to the pan with the honey and cook for 2-3 minutes until the porridge starts to thicken. Add the carrot to the porridge together with the remaining hemp milk and the salt and continue cooking for a further 2-3 minutes. Remove the pan from the heat and leave to stand for 2-3 minutes before pouring into a bowl.

Serve the porridge with the toppings.

SEA BUCKTHORN + RYE

200ml [scant 1 cup]	almond milk [see page 27]
15g [1 tbsp]	rye flakes
20g [$\frac{1}{4}$ cup]	rolled oats
$\frac{1}{2}$ tsp	ground cinnamon
1 tsp	sea buckthorn berry powder
1 tbsp	ground flaxseeds
$\frac{2}{3}$	large, fresh banana, mashed
pinch	salt

TOPPINGS

2 tbsp	homemade date 'chutney' [see page 133]
1 tbsp	fresh raspberries
1 tbsp	fresh sea buckthorn berries or cranberries
1 tbsp	fresh blackcurrants
1 tsp	nut butter of choice

MAKES 1 BOWL

Heat 100ml [7 tbsp] water and 100ml [7 tbsp] of the almond milk in a small saucepan until almost boiling.

Meanwhile, mix the rye, oats, cinnamon, berry powder and flaxseeds together in a small bowl, then add them to the milk. Stir, reduce the heat and cook for 2–3 minutes until the porridge starts to thicken. Add the banana and the remaining almond milk, stir and cook for a further 2 minutes until the banana has combined into the mixture. Add the salt and stir once more. Remove from the heat, cover with a lid and leave to stand for a couple of minutes.

Pour the porridge into a serving bowl and top with the date 'chutney', raspberries, sea buckthorn berries, blackcurrants and a spoonful of nut butter.

1 tbsp	ground flaxseeds
1 tsp	raw cacao powder
1 tsp	carob powder
1 tsp	maca powder [optional]
pinch	vanilla powder
200ml [scant 1 cup]	almond milk [see page 27]
70g [½ cup]	quinoa, rinsed
1 tsp	coconut butter [manna]
pinch	salt
⅔	large, fresh banana, mashed

+ TOPPINGS

1 serving	raspberry banana 'ice cream' [see page 129]
1 tbsp	fresh blackcurrants
1 tbsp	fresh sea buckthorn berries or cranberries
1 tbsp	desiccated coconut
1 tsp	dried goji berries
1 tsp	cacao nibs

MAKES 1 BOWL

Mix the flaxseeds, cacao, carob, maca [if using] and vanilla together in a small bowl.

Bring 100ml [7 tbsp] water and 100ml [7 tbsp] of the almond milk to the boil in a small saucepan. Reduce the heat to low and add the quinoa, coconut butter and flaxseeds mixture to the pan. Add the salt then cook, stirring occasionally, for 5 minutes. Add the banana to the pan, then add the remaining almond milk. Stir and cook for a further 5-7 minutes. Remove the pan from the heat and pour the porridge into a serving bowl.

Serve with the toppings.

DOUBLE CHOCOLATE
+ QUINOA

SPICED APPLE, PEANUT BUTTER + JELLY

1	large, fresh apple, washed
35g [scant ½ cup]	rolled oats
1 tbsp	ground flaxseeds
½ tsp	ground cinnamon
½ tsp	ground cardamom
1 tsp	ginger juice or ½ tsp grated ginger
1 tsp	peanut butter
200ml [scant 1 cup]	almond milk [see page 27]

+ TOPPINGS

2 tbsp	blackcurrant + vanilla chia 'jam' [see page 134]
1 tbsp	dried figs, roughly chopped
1 tbsp	fresh cloudberries or cranberries
1 tbsp	fresh lingonberries or raspberries
1 tsp	nut butter of choice
1 tsp	dried flower sprinkle [optional]

MAKES 1 BOWL

The night before, grate the apple and put it into an airtight jar or container. Mix the oats, flaxseeds, cinnamon and cardamom together in a bowl and add the mixture to the grated apple. Combine the ginger juice, peanut butter and almond milk in a small bowl, then add to the jar or container. Mix well, then cover and chill the porridge overnight in the fridge.

In the morning, heat the porridge quickly in a small saucepan over a medium heat until it becomes soft. Turn off the heat, cover with a lid and leave to stand for a couple of minutes before pouring into a serving bowl.

Top the porridge with the 'jam', dried figs, fresh berries, nut butter and a sprinkle of dried flowers, if using.

35g [⅓ cup]	quinoa flakes
1 tbsp	chia seeds
1 tsp	maca powder
½ tsp	vanilla powder
200ml [scant 1 cup]	almond milk [see page 27]
pinch	salt
1	large, fresh banana, mashed

✛ TOPPINGS

1 tbsp	fresh raspberries
1 tbsp	fresh sea buckthorn berries or cranberries
1 tbsp	fresh blackcurrants
1 tbsp	dried mulberries
½ tbsp	coconut flakes
1 tsp	bee pollen [optional]
1 tsp	nut butter of choice

MAKES 1 BOWL

Mix the quinoa flakes, chia seeds, maca powder and vanilla together in a bowl.

Bring 100ml [7 tbsp] water and 100ml [7 tbsp] of the almond milk to the boil in a small saucepan. Reduce the heat and add the quinoa mixture to the pan. Add the salt and cook, stirring occasionally, for about 3 minutes. Add the banana, then add the remaining almond milk. Stir and cook for a further 2–3 minutes.

Remove the pan from the heat, pour the porridge into a serving bowl and top with the berries, coconut, bee pollen [if using] and a spoonful of nut butter.

THE SUPERFOODIE

200ml [scant 1 cup]	oat milk
35g [scant $\frac{1}{2}$ cup]	rolled oats
$\frac{1}{2}$ tsp	ground cardamom
1 tsp	blueberry powder or 100ml [scant $\frac{1}{2}$ cup] fresh blueberries
1 tbsp	ground flaxseeds
$\frac{2}{3}$	large, fresh banana, mashed
pinch	salt

✚ TOPPINGS

$\frac{1}{3}$	large, fresh banana, sliced
2 tbsp	fresh blueberries or bilberries
2 tbsp	fresh raspberries
1 tbsp	dried inca berries [optional]
$\frac{1}{2}$ tbsp	black tahini [see page 138]
1 tsp	dried flower sprinkle [optional]

MAKES 1 BOWL

Bring 100ml [7 tbsp] water and 100ml [7 tbsp] of the oat milk to the boil in a small saucepan.

Meanwhile, mix the oats, cardamom, berry powder and flaxseeds together in a bowl, then add them to the oat milk. Stir, reduce the heat and cook for 2-3 minutes until the porridge starts to thicken. Add the banana and the remaining oat milk, stir and cook for a further 2 minutes until the banana has combined into the mixture. Add the salt and stir once more.

Remove the pan from the heat, cover with a lid and leave to stand for a couple of minutes. Pour the porridge into a serving bowl and top with banana, berries, tahini and a sprinkle of dried flowers, if using.

BLUEBERRY + CARDAMOM

RAW BUCKWHEAT, CACAO + NECTARINE

70g [scant ½ cup]	raw buckwheat groats
100ml [7 tbsp]	cinnamon cashew milk [see page 31]
1 tbsp	nut milk pulp [optional]
3	small, fresh nectarines, stoned and chopped
1 tbsp	whole flaxseeds
1 tsp	raw cacao powder

+ **TOPPINGS**

1 tbsp	fresh cloudberries or raspberries
1 tbsp	fresh lingonberries or cranberries
1 tbsp	fresh blackcurrants
½ tbsp	cacao nibs
1 tbsp	coconut flakes

MAKES 1 BOWL

The night before, rinse then soak the buckwheat in a bowl of water.

In the morning, rinse the buckwheat well in fresh water, then place in a high-speed blender with all the remaining ingredients and blend together until smooth.

Serve the porridge with the toppings.

APPLE MULTIGRAIN BIRCHER

1	large, fresh apple, cored and grated
1½ tbsp	rolled oats
1 tbsp	spelt flakes
1 tbsp	rye flakes
1 tbsp	chia seeds
1 tbsp	dried sour cherries or cranberries
½ tsp	ground cinnamon
150ml [10 tbsp]	oat milk
100ml [7 tbsp]	nut 'rawgurt' [see page 36] or unsweetened soy yogurt

+ TOPPINGS

3 tbsp	blackcurrant + vanilla chia 'jam' [see page 134]
1 tbsp	fresh raspberries
1 tbsp	fresh cloudberries or cranberries
1 tsp	crushed liquorice almonds [see page 130]
1 tsp	dried flower sprinkle [optional]

MAKES 1 BOWL

The night before, place the apple in an airtight jar or container. Mix the grains, chia seeds, sour cherries and cinnamon together in a bowl, then add the mixture to the apple.

Mix the oat milk and nut 'rawgurt' together in a small bowl, then pour into the jar and mix well. Cover and chill overnight in the fridge.

In the morning, stir and pour the bircher muesli into a serving bowl. Top with the 'jam', fresh berries, almonds and a sprinkle of dried flowers, if using.

RAW BUCKWHEAT, BLACKCURRANT + LIQUORICE

70g [scant $\frac{1}{2}$ cup]	raw buckwheat groats
100ml [7 tbsp]	oat milk
100g [1 cup]	fresh blackcurrants
1	large, fresh banana
1 tbsp	ground flaxseeds
$\frac{1}{4}$ tsp	liquorice root powder
$\frac{1}{2}$ tsp	ashwagandha [optional]

+ TOPPINGS

1 tbsp	fresh blackcurrants
1 tbsp	fresh raspberries
1 tbsp	fresh cloudberries or cranberries
1 tbsp	dried mulberries
$\frac{1}{2}$ tbsp	black tahini [see page 138]

MAKES 1 BOWL

The night before, rinse then soak the buckwheat in a bowl of water.

In the morning, rinse the buckwheat well in fresh water, then place in a high-speed blender with all the remaining ingredients and blend together until smooth.

Serve the porridge with the toppings.

35g [⅓ cup]	quinoa flakes
1 tbsp	chia seeds
½ tbsp	raw cacao powder
½	large, fresh banana
200ml [scant 1 cup]	cinnamon cashew milk [see page 31]

 TOPPINGS

1 serving	matcha banana 'ice cream' [see page 126]
1 tbsp	freeze-dried raspberries
½ tbsp	cacao nibs
1 tbsp	coconut flakes

MAKES 1 JAR OR 400 ML [2 CUPS]

The night before, mix all the dry ingredients together in a glass jar. Blend the banana and cashew milk together in a high-speed blender, then pour into the jar. Mix well, cover and chill overnight in the fridge.

In the morning, prepare the banana 'ice cream', then place a scoop on top of the jar and decorate with the raspberries, cacao nibs and coconut flakes.

CACAO + QUINOA JAR

PEAR
+ CHAI
BIRCHER

1	large, fresh pear, washed and cored
35g [scant ½ cup]	rolled oats
1 tbsp	ground flaxseeds
½ tsp	ground cinnamon
½ tsp	ground cardamom
pinch	ground nutmeg
200ml [scant 1 cup]	cinnamon cashew milk [see page 31]

+ TOPPINGS

2 tbsp	homemade date 'chutney' [see page 133]
1 tbsp	fresh blueberries
1 tbsp	fresh lingonberries or cranberries
1 tsp	crushed liquorice almonds [see page 130]
1 tsp	dried flower sprinkle [optional]
½	large, fresh pear, washed, cored and finely sliced

MAKES 1 BOWL

The night before, grate the pear into small pieces and put into a glass jar. Mix the oats, flaxseeds, cinnamon, cardamom and nutmeg together in a small bowl, then add to the pear. Pour in the cashew milk and mix well. Cover and chill overnight in the fridge.

In the morning, stir and pour the bircher muesli into a serving bowl. Top with the date 'chutney', berries, almonds, a sprinkle of dried flowers [if using] and a few slices of pear.

BOTTOM LAYER

1 tbsp	chia seeds
1 tsp	raw cacao powder
1 tsp	carob powder
50ml [3½ tbsp]	oat milk

MIDDLE LAYER

35g [scant ½ cup]	rolled oats
1 tbsp	chia seeds
1 tbsp	dried sour cherries or dried cranberries
½ tsp	ground cinnamon
100ml [7 tbsp]	nut 'rawgurt' [see page 36] or unsweetened soy yogurt
150ml [10 tbsp]	oat milk

TOPPINGS

1 serving	raspberry banana 'ice cream' [see page 129]
1 tbsp	freeze-dried strawberries
1 tbsp	coconut flakes
½ tbsp	dried flower sprinkle [optional]

MAKES 1 JAR OR 400 ML [2 CUPS]

The night before, for the bottom layer, mix the chia seeds, cacao, carob and oat milk together in a glass jar. Stir, then cover and chill overnight in the fridge.

In a separate glass jar, mix all the dry ingredients for the middle layer together. Combine the 'rawgurt' and oat milk in a bowl, then add to the dry ingredients and mix together. Stir and chill overnight in the fridge.

In the morning, arrange the middle layer on top of the bottom layer, then prepare the banana 'ice cream' and add a scoop on top. Decorate with freeze-dried strawberries, coconut flakes and a sprinkle of dried flowers, if using.

CHOCOLATE BERRY JAR

RAW BUCKWHEAT,
APPLE + CINNAMON

70g [scant ½ cup]	raw buckwheat groats
100ml [7 tbsp]	cinnamon cashew milk [see page 31]
1	large, fresh apple, cored and chopped
1 tbsp	nut milk pulp [optional]
1 tbsp	whole flaxseeds
½ tsp	ground cinnamon

+ TOPPINGS

1 tbsp	fresh blackcurrants
1 tbsp	fresh raspberries
1 tbsp	fresh cloudberries or cranberries
1 tbsp	dried figs, roughly chopped
½ tbsp	crushed liquorice almonds [see page 130]

MAKES 1 BOWL

The night before, rinse then soak the buckwheat in a bowl of water at room temperature.

In the morning, rinse the buckwheat well in fresh water, then place in a high-speed blender with all the remaining ingredients and blend together until smooth.

Serve the porridge with the toppings.

BOTTOM LAYER

1 tbsp	chia seeds
$\frac{1}{2}$ tsp	ground turmeric
$\frac{1}{2}$ tsp	honey, or coconut nectar for a vegan option
50ml [3$\frac{1}{2}$ tbsp]	oat milk

MIDDLE LAYER

35g [scant $\frac{1}{2}$ cup]	rolled oats
1 tbsp	chia seeds
1 tbsp	dried mulberries
$\frac{1}{2}$ tsp	vanilla powder
100ml [7 tbsp]	nut 'rawgurt' [see page 36] or unsweetened soy yogurt
150ml [10 tbsp]	oat milk

+ TOPPINGS

1 serving	matcha banana 'ice cream' [see page 126]
1 tbsp	freeze-dried blueberries
1 tbsp	coconut flakes
$\frac{1}{2}$ tsp	bee pollen [optional]

MAKES 1 JAR OR 400 ML [2 CUPS]

The night before, for the bottom layer, mix the chia seeds, turmeric, honey or coconut nectar and oat milk together in a glass jar. Stir, then cover and chill overnight in the fridge.

In a separate glass jar, mix all the dry ingredients together for the middle layer. Combine the liquids in a bowl, then add to the jar and stir together to combine. Cover and chill overnight in the fridge.

In the morning, prepare the banana 'ice cream' and add a scoop on top. Decorate with the freeze-dried berries, coconut and a sprinkle of bee pollen, if using.

TURMERIC, MULBERRY + VANILLA JAR

RAW BUCKWHEAT, BLUEBERRY + CARDAMOM

70g [scant $\frac{1}{2}$ cup]	raw buckwheat groats
100ml [7 tbsp]	oat milk
100g [scant 1 cup]	fresh blueberries or bilberries
1	large, fresh banana
1 tbsp	ground flaxseeds
$\frac{1}{2}$ tsp	ground cardamom
$\frac{1}{2}$ tsp	reishi [optional]

+ **TOPPINGS**

1 tbsp	fresh blueberries or bilberries
1 tbsp	fresh raspberries
1 tbsp	fresh sea buckthorn berries or cranberries
1 tbsp	coconut flakes

MAKES 1 BOWL

The night before, rinse then soak the buckwheat in a bowl of water at room temperature.

In the morning, rinse the buckwheat well in fresh water, then place in a high-speed blender with all the remaining ingredients and blend together until smooth.

Serve the porridge with the toppings.

Reishi is an adaptogenic mushroom known for reducing stress and improving your sleep quality. Reishi also has immune-boosting and hormone-balancing qualities. Take it in small doses.

PEAR +
LIQUORICE
BIRCHER

1	large, fresh pear, washed and cored
35g [scant ½ cup]	rolled oats
1 tbsp	chia seeds
⅓ tsp	liquorice root powder
200ml [scant 1 cup]	vanilla hemp milk [see page 28]

+ **TOPPINGS**

1	dried fig, roughly chopped
1 tbsp	fresh blueberries
1 tbsp	fresh raspberries
1 tbsp	fresh sea buckthorn berries or cranberries
1 tsp	black tahini [see page 138]
few slices	large, fresh pear, washed and cored

MAKES 1 BOWL

The night before, chop the pear into small pieces and put in a glass jar. Mix the oats, chia seeds and liquorice powder together in a bowl, then add to the pear and mix well. Add the vanilla hemp milk and mix well. Cover and chill overnight in the fridge.

In the morning, pour the muesli into a bowl and top with the fig, berries, a spoonful of tahini and a few pear slices.

BEETROOT + LIQUORICE BOWL

1	large, fresh banana
1	medium beetroot [beet], cut into cubes, steamed and chilled
120g [1 cup]	frozen lingonberries or cranberries
$\frac{1}{3}$ tsp	liquorice powder
$\frac{1}{2}$ tsp	ashwagandha [optional]
150ml [10 tbsp]	nut 'rawgurt' [see page 36] or unsweetened soy yogurt

+ TOPPINGS

120g [$\frac{1}{2}$ cup}	fresh berries of your choice
few slices	rainbow beetroot [beet], thinly sliced into triangles or half moons
1 serving	cacao + goji sprinkle [see page 122]
1 tsp	chia seeds
1 tsp	cacao nibs
1 tsp	desiccated coconut
1 tsp	goji berries

MAKES 1 BOWL

Blitz all the ingredients, except the toppings, together in a high-speed blender. Pour into a bowl and create smoothie bowl art on top with the toppings!

Ashwagandha is an adaptogenic herb and it's also a well-known aphrodisiac which is used in Indian medicine to improve both mental and physical stamina, which helps to relieve stress and fatigue. Take it in small doses.

NORDIC AÇAÍ BOWL

1	large, fresh banana [reserve a few slices for the topping]
70g [scant $\frac{1}{2}$ cup]	frozen blueberries or bilberries
70g [scant $\frac{3}{4}$ cup]	frozen blackcurrants
1 tsp	açaí powder
150ml [10 tbsp]	nut 'rawgurt' [see page 36] or unsweetened soy yogurt

TOPPINGS

3 tbsp	fresh berries of your choice
1 serving	pistachio + fig sprinkle [see page 117]
1 tsp	chia seeds
1 tsp	cacao nibs
1 tsp	desiccated coconut
1 tsp	bee pollen [optional]

MAKES 1 BOWL

Blitz all the ingredients, except the toppings, together in a high-speed blender. Pour into a bowl and make smoothie bowl art on top with the toppings!

COURGETTE, CACAO + BERRY BOWL

1	small ripe avocado, peeled and pitted
100g [1 cup]	frozen raspberries
50g [$\frac{1}{4}$ cup]	frozen lingonberries or cranberries
$\frac{1}{2}$	small courgette [zucchini], roughly chopped
1 tsp	raw cacao powder
2	dates, pitted
150ml [10 tbsp]	nut 'rawgurt' [see page 36] or unsweetened soy yogurt

+ | **TOPPINGS**

3 tbsp	fresh berries of your choice
1 serving	pistachio + fig sprinkle [see page 117]
1 tsp	hemp hearts
1 tsp	chia seeds
1 tsp	desiccated coconut
1 tsp	bee pollen [optional]

MAKES 1 BOWL

Blitz all the ingredients, except the toppings, together in a high-speed blender. Pour into a bowl and make smoothie bowl art on top with the toppings!

GREEN
POWDER
BOWL

1	large, fresh banana [reserve a few slices for the topping]
3	cubes frozen baby spinach or two large handfuls of fresh spinach
120g [4¼ oz]	frozen edamame beans
juice of ¼	lemon
1 tsp	wheatgrass powder
150ml [10 tbsp]	nut 'rawgurt' [see page 36] or unsweetened soy yogurt

+

TOPPINGS

3 tbsp	fresh berries of your choice
1 serving	cacao + goji sprinkle [see page 122]
1 tsp	chia seeds
1 tsp	cacao nibs
1 tsp	desiccated coconut
1 tsp	bee pollen [optional]

MAKES 1 BOWL

Blitz all the ingredients, except the toppings, together in a high-speed blender. Pour into a bowl and make smoothie bowl art on top with the toppings!

MERMAID BOWL

1	large, fresh apple [such as granny smith or another crisp variety], cut into cubes and frozen
½	medium ripe avocado, peeled and pitted
1 tsp	spirulina powder
few drops	peppermint essential oil
150ml [10 tbsp]	nut 'rawgurt' [see page 36] or unsweetened soy yogurt

+ **TOPPINGS**

3 tbsp	fresh berries of your choice
few	fresh mint leaves
1 serving	sesame + coconut 'rawnola' [see page 124]
1 tsp	cacao nibs
1 tsp	desiccated coconut
1 tsp	bee pollen [optional]

MAKES 1 BOWL

Blitz all the ingredients, except the toppings, together in a high-speed blender with 50ml [3½ tbsp] water. Pour into a bowl and make smoothie bowl art on top with the toppings!

SAVOURY

THREE-GRAIN, GREENS + ZA'ATAR

2	chia 'eggs' [see page 33]
$\frac{1}{2}$ tbsp	sesame oil
1	small shallot, chopped
1 tsp	za'atar
handful	spinach, washed
$1\frac{1}{2}$ tbsp	rolled oats
$\frac{3}{4}$ tbsp	spelt flakes
$\frac{3}{4}$ tbsp	rye flakes
pinch	salt

+ TOPPINGS

$\frac{1}{2}$ tbsp	sesame oil
150g [5$\frac{1}{4}$ oz]	broccoli, cut into large chunks
$\frac{1}{2}$ tbsp	raw apple cider vinegar
$\frac{1}{4}$	large, ripe avocado, peeled, pitted and cut into slices
handful	flat-leaf parsley, chopped

MAKES 1 BOWL

First prepare the chia 'eggs'.

Next, heat the sesame oil over a medium-high heat in a small saucepan, add the shallot and za'atar and fry for 2–3 minutes until soft. Add the spinach and sauté lightly until it's wilted, then reduce the heat and add the oats, spelt, rye and 200ml [scant 1 cup] water. Cook for about 5 minutes, stirring occasionally until the grains have softened. Finally, add the chia 'eggs' and continue cooking for a further 3–4 minutes until they have dissolved. Add a pinch of salt to taste, then remove the porridge from the heat, cover and keep warm while you prepare the toppings.

Blanch the broccoli quickly in boiling water, then rinse with cold water. Season with sesame oil, salt and vinegar. Pour the porridge into a bowl and top with broccoli, avocado slices and parsley.

½ tbsp	sesame oil
1	small red onion, chopped
½ tsp	smoked paprika
½ tsp	chilli flakes
80g [½ cup]	amaranth
150g [5½ oz]	butternut squash, peeled, deseeded and cut into cubes
pinch	salt

+ TOPPINGS

1 serving	garlic sautéed spinach [see page 144]
100g [¾ cup]	canned or cooked sweetcorn, rinsed and drained
150g [1 cup]	canned or cooked black beans, rinsed and drained
¼	large, ripe avocado, peeled, pitted and cut into slices
sprinkle	black sesame seeds

MAKES 1 BOWL

For the topping, prepare the garlic sautéed spinach.

Next, heat the sesame oil over a medium-high heat in a small saucepan, add the onion and spices and fry for 2–3 minutes. Rinse the amaranth and add to the pan together with 300ml [1¼ cups] water. Reduce the heat and cook for about 20 minutes, stirring occasionally.

Meanwhile, steam the butternut squash until soft, then blend it with a stick blender to a purée. Add to the amaranth porridge and stir to combine. Add the salt, then continue cooking for a further 5 minutes. Pour the porridge into a serving bowl and add the toppings.

AMARANTH,
BLACK BEANS + CORN

½ tbsp	sesame oil
1	small red onion, chopped
1 tsp	brown rice miso paste
80g [½ cup]	amaranth
150g [5½ oz]	butternut squash, peeled, deseeded and cut into cubes

+ **TOPPINGS**

1 tsp	sesame oil
100g [3½ oz]	smoked tempeh, cut into slices
1 tsp	tamari
handful	my favourite tahini kale [see page 140]
1 tbsp	my standard pickles [see page 146]

MAKES 1 BOWL

Heat the sesame oil over a medium-high heat in a saucepan. Add the onion and brown rice miso and fry for 2–3 minutes until the onion is soft. Rinse the amaranth and add it to the pan with 300ml [1¼ cups] water. Reduce the heat to medium and slowly let the amaranth cook for 20 minutes, stirring occasionally.

Meanwhile, prepare the toppings. Heat the sesame oil in a pan, add the tempeh and fry it lightly with a splash of tamari for 5–7 minutes until it turns golden. Set aside.

For the porridge, steam the butternut squash until soft, then blend it with a stick blender to a purée. Add to the amaranth porridge, stir in and cook for a further 3–5 minutes.

Remove the porridge from the heat and pour into a serving bowl. Top with the tahini kale, smoked tempeh and some pickled red cabbage.

AMARANTH, BUTTERNUT
+ SMOKED TEMPEH

AMARANTH, COURGETTE + SHISHO

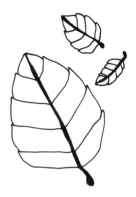

½ tbsp	sesame oil
¼ tsp	garlic powder
½ tsp	ginger, grated
½ tsp	brown rice miso paste
80g [½ cup]	amaranth
50g [1¾ oz]	courgette [zucchini]
½ tbsp	brown rice vinegar
120g [4¼ oz]	frozen edamame beans, thawed and cooked

+   **TOPPINGS**

handful	kale, sliced
½ tbsp	sesame oil
½ tbsp	tamari
1	shisho leaf, washed in hot water
1	slice of lemon

MAKES 1 BOWL

Heat the sesame oil, garlic, ginger and miso over a medium-high heat in a saucepan. Rinse the amaranth and add it to the pan with 300ml [1¼ cups] water. Reduce the heat to medium and slowly let the amaranth cook for 20 minutes, stirring occasionally.

Meanwhile, grate the courgette, then add it to the amaranth together with the brown rice vinegar and cook for a further 5 minutes. Add the edamame beans and remove the pan from the heat.

For the toppings, blanch the kale quickly in boiling water [a couple of seconds is enough], then rinse in cold water, drain and, using your hands, massage the leaves with the sesame oil and tamari.

Pour the porridge into a serving bowl, top with the kale, a shisho leaf and a slice of lemon.

BLACK RICE, MISO + SHIITAKE

80g [½ cup]	black rice
100ml [7 tbsp]	coconut milk
½ tsp	brown rice miso paste
1 tsp	sesame oil
150g [5½ oz]	sweet potato, peeled and grated

+

TOPPINGS

1 tsp	sesame oil
100g [3½ oz]	shiitake mushrooms, sliced
½ tbsp	tamari
100g [3½ oz]	broccoli, chopped into small chunks
1 serving	edamame 'hummus' [see page 152]

MAKES 1 BOWL

Put the black rice, 200ml [scant 1 cup] water, coconut milk, miso paste and sesame oil into a small saucepan and bring to the boil. Reduce the heat to medium and continue cooking for about 25 minutes, stirring occasionally. Add the sweet potato and cook for a further 5–10 minutes. Stir, then remove the pan from the heat and leave to stand for a couple of minutes.

While the porridge is cooking, prepare your toppings. Heat the sesame oil over a medium-high heat in a large saucepan, add the shiitake mushrooms and tamari and stir-fry for a couple of minutes until lightly browned. Remove the shiitake mushrooms from the pan and add the broccoli [don't wash the pan] and stir-fry for 1–2 minutes until it has a tiny bit of colour. Remove the pan from the heat, cover and steam for 3–4 minutes for a crunchy texture.

Serve the porridge with all the toppings.

BROWN RICE, GREENS + EDAMAME BEANS

1 tsp	sesame oil
2 tsp	ginger, grated
$\frac{1}{4}$ tsp	garlic powder
80g [$\frac{1}{2}$ cup]	brown rice
100ml [7 tbsp]	coconut milk
50g [1$\frac{1}{2}$ oz]	firm tofu
$\frac{1}{2}$ tbsp	tamari
1 tbsp	fresh coriander [cilantro], finely chopped
1 tbsp	spring onion [scallion], finely chopped
pinch	salt

+ TOPPINGS

handful	kale, sliced
1 tbsp	microgreens
60g [2$\frac{1}{4}$ oz]	frozen edamame beans, thawed and cooked
1 tbsp	spring onion [scallion], finely chopped
1 tbsp	dried nori seaweed, cut into strips

MAKES 1 BOWL

Heat the sesame oil over a medium-high heat in a saucepan, add the ginger, garlic and rice and fry until golden. Pour in 300ml [1$\frac{1}{4}$ cups] water and a sprinkle of salt and cook the rice for 40 minutes, stirring occasionally. Pour in the coconut milk and continue to cook for a further 20 minutes. Add the tofu, tamari, coriander and spring onion, stir, then remove the pan from the heat and cover for a couple of minutes before pouring the porridge into a serving bowl.

For the toppings, blanch the kale quickly in boiling water [a couple of seconds], then rinse in cold water and drain.

Top the porridge with the kale, microgreens, edamame beans, spring onion and nori strips.

BUCKWHEAT, BEETROOT PESTO + CASHEW 'CHEEZE'

70g [$\frac{1}{2}$ cup]	raw buckwheat groats, well rinsed
1 tsp	sesame oil
$\frac{1}{2}$ tsp	ground coriander
$\frac{1}{3}$ tsp	garlic powder
pinch	salt

+ TOPPINGS

1 tsp	sesame oil
100g [$3\frac{1}{2}$ oz]	smoked tempeh, crumbled
1 serving	beetroot + pumpkin 'pesto' [see page 148]
1 serving	garlic sautéed spinach [see page 144]
1 serving	cashew cream 'cheeze' [see page 150]

MAKES 1 BOWL

Heat 200ml [scant 1 cup] water in a small saucepan until it is almost boiling, then reduce the heat and add the buckwheat, sesame oil, coriander, garlic and salt. Cook for 10–12 minutes until almost all the water has been absorbed, then pour in 50ml [$3\frac{1}{2}$ tbsp] water and cook for a further 3–5 minutes. Remove from the heat and cover with a lid.

Heat the sesame oil over a medium-high heat in a small frying pan, add the tempeh and pan-fry lightly until coloured. Mix the pesto into the porridge, then pour the porridge into a serving bowl and top with the smoked tempeh, a spoonful of cashew 'cheeze' and a good amount of the sautéed spinach on top.

OATS, KALE, TOFU + SWEET POTATO

100ml [7 tbsp]	cinnamon cashew milk [see page 31]
35g [scant ½ cup]	rolled oats
1 tsp	coconut oil
2	chia 'eggs' [see page 33]
¼ tsp	garlic powder
pinch	salt

+ TOPPINGS

120g [4¼ oz]	firm tofu
1 serving	kale + cashew 'pesto' [see page 148]
½	small sweet potato, peeled and cut into cubes
1 serving	hemp heart 'parmesan' [see page 150]

MAKES 1 BOWL

Bring the cinnamon cashew milk and 100ml [7 tbsp] water in a small saucepan to the boil, then reduce the heat to low, and add the oats, coconut oil, garlic and salt. Cook for about 5 minutes, stirring occasionally. Add the chia 'eggs' and stir constantly until the eggs are dissolved. Pour the porridge into a serving bowl and set aside.

Rinse the tofu and pat dry, then cut it into small cubes. Mix the kale 'pesto' into the tofu and set aside.

Steam the sweet potato until soft, then using a stick blender, blend it to a purée. Top the porridge with the sweet potato mash, kale tofu and hemp heart 'parmesan'.

QUINOA, BEETROOT + GINGER

70g [½ cup]	white quinoa, rinsed
1	small beetroot [beet], grated
1 tsp	ginger, grated
1 tsp	coconut butter [manna]
1 tbsp	brown rice vinegar
1	dried nori seaweed sheet
pinch	salt

+   **TOPPINGS**

¼	large, ripe avocado, peeled and pitted
pinch	wasabi powder
squeeze	lemon
125g [4¼ oz]	firm tofu
1 tsp	fresh coriander [cilantro], finely chopped

MAKES 1 BOWL

Put the quinoa into a small saucepan together with 300ml [1¼ cups] water, add the beetroot, ginger and coconut butter and cook for about 10–15 minutes on a low heat. Remove from the heat and leave until completely cool. When the porridge is cold, add the vinegar and mix to combine.

To make a wasabi-avocado mousse for the topping, place the avocado flesh into a small bowl and use a fork to mash it into a smooth paste. In a small bowl, mix the wasabi powder with 1 tsp water and the lemon juice, then leave to stand until it becomes thick – about 2–3 minutes. Add the wasabi paste to the avocado and mix well to combine.

Rinse the tofu and pat dry, then crumble it into tiny pieces and stir it into the wasabi-avocado mousse. Cut the nori sheet into 4 triangles and place in the base of a serving bowl. Top with the beetroot and ginger quinoa, wasabi-avocado and coriander. Eat with either a spoon or chopsticks!

QUINOA, SWEET POTATO + EDAMAME

1	shallot, chopped
1 tsp	coconut oil
$\frac{1}{2}$ tsp	ground turmeric
pinch	cayenne pepper
70g [$\frac{1}{2}$ cup]	quinoa, rinsed
150g [$5\frac{1}{2}$ oz]	sweet potato, peeled and grated
100ml [7 tbsp]	almond milk [see page 27]
pinch	salt

+ TOPPINGS

120g [$4\frac{1}{4}$ oz]	frozen edamame beans, thawed and cooked
1 tbsp	alfalfa sprouts
2 tbsp	my standard pickles [see page 146]
1 serving	my favourite tahini kale [see page 140]

MAKES 1 BOWL

Put the shallot into a small saucepan together with the coconut oil and spices. Fry, on a medium heat, for 1–2 minutes until the shallot softens, then add the quinoa, 200ml [scant 1 cup] water and the sweet potato. Reduce the heat and cook for about 10 minutes until almost all the liquid has been absorbed. Add the almond milk and continue cooking for a further 5 minutes. Add salt to taste, then remove the porridge from the heat, cover and leave to stand for a couple of minutes.

Top the porridge with the edamame beans, alfalfa, pickles and tahini kale.

SIMPLE OATS, KALE + CARROT BACON

100ml [7 tbsp]	oat milk
35g [scant $\frac{1}{2}$ cup]	rolled oats
1 tsp	coconut oil
$\frac{1}{4}$ tsp	garlic powder
pinch	salt
2	chia 'eggs' [see page 33]

+

TOPPINGS

1 serving	my favourite tahini kale [see page 140]
1 serving	carrot 'bacon' [see page 143]
sprinkle	black sesame seeds
$\frac{1}{4}$	large, ripe avocado, peeled, pitted and cut into slices

MAKES 1 BOWL

Bring the oat milk and 100ml [7 tbsp] water to the boil in a small saucepan. Reduce the heat, then add the oats, coconut oil, garlic and salt and cook for about 5 minutes, stirring occasionally until the mixture thickens. Add the chia 'eggs' and continue stirring until they are dissolved. Transfer the porridge to a serving bowl and serve with all the toppings.

TOPPINGS

PISTACHIO
+ FIG
SPRINKLE

TOASTED

240g [1½ cups]	raw buckwheat groats, rinsed
1 tsp	ground cardamom
1 tsp	ground cinnamon
1–2 tbsp	coconut oil, melted
80g [1 cup]	rolled oats
50g [⅓ cup]	pistachios, shelled and chopped
35g [scant ¼ cup]	whole flaxseeds
35g [¼ cup]	sesame seeds
50g [scant ½ cup]	dried sour cherries or cranberries
50g [⅓ cup]	dried figs, roughly chopped

MAKES 1 LARGE JAR OR 1L [4½ CUPS]

Preheat the oven to 180°C/350°F/Gas 4 and line a baking tray with parchment paper.

Mix the buckwheat, cardamom and cinnamon together in a bowl, then spread the mixture out on the prepared baking tray and drizzle with the melted coconut oil. Mix until coated then spread out again and bake in the oven for about 15–20 minutes, stirring occasionally. Keep an eye on the mixture as it may burn.

Meanwhile, mix all the 'raw' ingredients together in a large bowl. Remove the toasted mixture from the oven, leave to cool, then combine it with the 'raw' ingredients.

Store in an airtight jar for up to 4 weeks.

	TOASTED
80g [scant 1 cup]	quinoa flakes
40g [½ cup]	rolled oats
1-2 tbsp	coconut oil, melted
1 tsp	ground turmeric
1 tsp	ground cinnamon
1 tsp	ground ginger
80g [1 cup]	rolled oats
60g [½ cup]	hazelnuts, roughly chopped
30g [¾ cup]	coconut flakes
35g [¼ cup]	pumpkin seeds
35g [¼ cup]	sesame seeds
50g [scant ½ cup]	dried sour cherries or cranberries
50g [scant ½ cup]	dried inca berries

MAKES 1 LARGE JAR OR 1L [4½ CUPS]

Preheat the oven to 180°C/350°F/Gas 4 and line a baking tray with parchment paper.

For the toasted ingredients, mix the quinoa flakes, oats, coconut oil, turmeric, cinnamon and ginger together in a bowl. Spread the quinoa mixture out on the prepared baking tray and bake in the oven for about 15-20 minutes, or until golden and fragrant. Remove from the oven and leave to cool.

Mix all the 'raw' ingredients together in a bowl, add the toasted quinoa mixture and stir to combine.

Store in an airtight jar for up to 4 weeks.

TURMERIC +
QUINOA SPRINKLE

CACAO +
GOJI SPRINKLE

TOASTED

80g [$\frac{1}{2}$ cup]	raw buckwheat groats, rinsed
80g [1 cup]	rolled oats, rye flakes, spelt flakes or a mix
1 tbsp	raw cacao powder
1–2 tbsp	coconut oil, melted

80g [1 cup]	rolled oats
60g [$\frac{1}{2}$ cup]	raw almonds, roughly chopped
35g [scant $\frac{1}{4}$ cup]	whole flaxseeds
35g [$\frac{1}{4}$ cup]	pumpkin seeds
50g [scant $\frac{1}{2}$ cup]	raw cacao nibs
50g [scant $\frac{1}{2}$ cup]	dried sour cherries or cranberries
50g [scant $\frac{1}{2}$ cup]	dried goji berries

MAKES 1 LARGE JAR
OR 1L [4 $\frac{1}{2}$ CUPS]

Preheat the oven to 180°C/350°F/Gas 4 and line a baking tray with parchment paper.

For the toasted ingredients, mix the buckwheat, the other grains of your choice and the cacao powder together in a bowl. Pour the mixture onto the prepared baking tray and drizzle with the melted coconut oil. Mix to combine, then spread out and bake in the oven for about 15–20 minutes, stirring occasionally. Keep an eye on it to prevent it burning.

Meanwhile, mix all the 'raw' ingredients in a large bowl. Remove the toasted mixture from the oven, leave to cool, then combine with the 'raw' ingredients.

Store in an airtight jar for up to 4 weeks.

SESAME + COCONUT 'RAWNOLA'

$\frac{1}{2}$	large, fresh banana, roughly chopped
35g [scant $\frac{1}{2}$ cup]	rolled oats
2 tbsp	sesame seeds
2 tbsp	desiccated coconut
2 tbsp	dried mulberries
$\frac{1}{2}$ tsp	vanilla powder

SERVES 1-2

Put all the ingredients in a high-speed blender or food processor and blend together until it is a sticky paste. Remove from the blender or processor and crumble it up into small chunks. Enjoy as 'rawnola' on top of yogurt or smoothie bowls.

Store in an airtight jar for up to 2 days.

MATCHA BANANA 'ICE CREAM'

2	kiwi fruits, peeled and cut into cubes
$\frac{1}{2}$	large, fresh banana, roughly chopped
squeeze	lemon
1 tsp	matcha [green tea] powder

SERVES 1

The night before, freeze the kiwi fruit cubes in a freezer-proof container.

In the morning, put the frozen kiwi in a high-speed blender with the remaining ingredients and blend until smooth.

RASPBERRY BANANA 'ICE CREAM'

200g [1⅔ cups]	frozen raspberries
½	large, fresh banana, roughly chopped
squeeze	lemon

SERVES 2

Just blend it all in a high-speed blender until smooth.

LIQUORICE ALMONDS

3 tsp	liquorice root powder
pinch	salt
100g [¾ cup]	raw almonds [with skin on]

MAKES 1 SMALL JAR OR 400ML [2 CUPS]

Preheat the oven to 200°C/400°F/Gas 6 and line a baking tray with parchment paper.

Mix 5 tsp water, 2 tsp of the liquorice root powder and the salt together in a small bowl. In another bowl, add the almonds, then pour in the liquorice mixture and mix until the almonds are coated. Spread the almonds out on the prepared baking tray and bake in the oven for 7 minutes.

Remove the almonds from the oven and leave to cool, then mix in the remaining liquorice root powder. Eat as a snack or use as a topping for any sweet porridge.

Store in an airtight jar for up to 4 weeks.

DATE 'CHUTNEY'

10	dates, pitted
$\frac{1}{2}$ **tsp**	ground cinnamon
$\frac{1}{2}$ **tsp**	orange peel, finely grated
pinch	salt

MAKES 1 JAR OR 400ML [2 CUPS]

Put the dates into a small saucepan with the cinnamon, orange peel and salt. Heat gently, watching carefully and when the dates begin to soften, start adding 200ml [scant 1 cup] water gradually, stirring constantly with a wooden spoon. Cook for 7–10 minutes until it becomes a sticky jam.

Store in a sterilized airtight jar and serve on top of porridge or use as a spread on bread.

Store in an airtight jar for 1–2 days.

1 tbsp	chia seeds
½ tsp	vanilla powder
50g [½ cup]	fresh blackcurrants [thawed if frozen]

SERVES 1-2

To make a chia gel, mix the chia seeds and 50ml [3½ tbsp] water together in a bowl, then leave to stand for 5-10 minutes, stirring occasionally until the mixture thickens. Add the vanilla and blackcurrants to the chia gel and mix with a fork until it is a jam-like consistency.

Store in the fridge, in an airtight jar, for 1-2 to days.

BLACKCURRANT +
VANILLA CHIA 'JAM'

LEFTOVER NUT + SEED BUTTER

300g [2½ cups] | raw nuts and seeds [such as pecans, cashews, almonds and pumpkin seeds]

pinch | salt [optional]

MAKES 1 JAR OR 400ML [2 CUPS]

Put the nuts and seeds into a high-speed blender and start processing on a medium–high speed for 2–3 minutes [depending on the strength of the machine, you might need a longer time]. Scrape down any nut butter from the sides of the blender and keep processing until it is a creamy consistency. Add the salt if you like and whizz one more time until smooth.

Store in the fridge for up to 2 weeks.

Nut butters are my favourite porridge topping and are also a great pre-workout snack to enjoy with apple slices or banana boats. It's simple to make nut butters at home and I usually use a mixture of the nuts I have in my storecupboard [pantry], such as almonds, pecans, cashews and pumpkin seeds. I prefer making raw nut butter so I don't roast the nuts before grinding them. I also like to add spices such as cinnamon or turmeric.

320g [2¼ cups]	black sesame seeds
3 tbsp	sesame oil or mild-flavoured oil
sprinkle	bee pollen [optional]

MAKES 1 JAR OR 400ML [2 CUPS]

Place the sesame seeds in a high-speed blender and whizz for 2–3 minutes until you have a paste. Add the sesame oil and whizz until completely smooth. Scrape down any sesame seed spread from the sides of the blender while processing. Add a bit more oil if necessary to reach a lighter consistency.

Put into a sterilized jar, cover and store in the fridge for up to 2 weeks.

 There are many different types of tahini, all of them vary in colour, taste and texture. My favourite is the light, runny, unsalted tahini although I sometimes buy the salted, creamier and darker tahini to enjoy as a snack or spread. If you use shop-bought tahini, try to purchase an organic one and check the ingredients list to make sure it doesn't contain additives.

BLACK TAHINI

MY FAVOURITE TAHINI KALE

100g [3½ oz]	kale, chopped and stalks removed
½ tbsp	light tahini
1 tsp	umeboshi vinegar or lemon juice
1 tbsp	nutritional yeast flakes

SERVES 1-2

Put the kale into a large bowl and drizzle over the tahini and vinegar. Using your hands, massage the tahini and vinegar into the kale until it becomes completely soft. Add the nutritional yeast and mix well with a fork or spoon.

CARROT 'BACON'

1 tbsp	coconut oil, melted
1 tsp	blackstrap molasses
$\frac{1}{4}$ tsp	ground cinnamon
$\frac{1}{4}$ tsp	ground ginger
$\frac{1}{4}$ tsp	smoked paprika
pinch	cayenne pepper
pinch	salt
2	large carrots, peeled and cut into long thin slices

SERVES 1–2

Preheat the oven to 200°C/400°F/Gas 6 and line a baking tray with parchment paper.

In a bowl, mix the coconut oil, molasses, spices and salt together into a 'marinade'. Spread the carrot slices out on the prepared baking tray and brush on both sides with the 'marinade'. Bake in the oven for 7–10 minutes until crispy.

Arrange the baked carrots on top of some kitchen paper to remove the excess oil before using.

Serve immediately.

GARLIC SAUTÉED SPINACH

$\frac{1}{2}$ **tbsp**	sesame oil
1	large garlic clove, crushed
200g [7oz]	baby spinach
squeeze	lemon
pinch	salt

SERVES 2

Heat the sesame oil over a medium-high heat in a large saucepan, add the garlic and quickly fry for 1 minute. Turn off the heat, wash the spinach and add it to the pan together with the lemon and salt and sauté for 2 minutes until the spinach is wilted. Drain any excess liquid.

500g [1lb 2oz]	red cabbage, shredded
2 tsp	salt
75ml [5 tbsp]	brown rice vinegar
50ml [3½ tbsp]	raw apple cider vinegar
2 tbsp	tamari
2 tbsp	mustard seeds

MAKES 1 JAR OR 400ML [2 CUPS]

Put the cabbage into a large bowl and pour in enough hot water to cover the cabbage completely. Add the salt, mix well and leave the cabbage to soak for 4 hours. Drain all the liquid from the cabbage and rinse to remove any excess salt.

To make the pickling liquid, mix the vinegars, tamari, mustard seeds and 300ml [1¼ cups] water together. Put the cabbage into a sterilized jar and add the pickling liquid. Cover and shake so that everything is evenly distributed. Chill in the fridge for at least 24 hours. The longer the cabbage has been pickling, the stronger the taste.

Store in a sterilized, airtight jar in the fridge for up to 2 weeks.

MY STANDARD PICKLES

KALE + CASHEW 'PESTO'

2 large handfuls	kale, stalks removed
handful	fresh basil
50g [scant $\frac{1}{2}$ cup]	cashews
$\frac{1}{3}$ tsp	garlic powder
juice of $\frac{1}{2}$	lemon
pinch	salt, to taste

SERVES 1-2

Put the kale into a high-speed blender together with the remaining ingredients and process. Start to add 2 tbsp water gradually until you reach your desired consistency. I like my kale pesto quite thick but you might want to add some more water to make it smoother.

Store in the fridge, in an airtight jar, for 1–2 days.

BEETROOT + PUMPKIN 'PESTO'

2	small beetroots [beet], washed and cut into cubes
2	sun-dried tomatoes, drained [4 halves]
handful	fresh basil
handful	fresh coriander [cilantro]
2 tbsp	pumpkin seeds
juice of $\frac{1}{2}$	lemon

SERVES 1-2

Steam or boil the beetroot until soft. If the sun-dried tomatoes are very dry, soak them in a small bowl of water for 5–10 minutes until soft, then drain. Put the cooked beetroot into a high-speed blender together with all the other ingredients, including the sun-dried tomatoes, and process until smooth. Add a splash of water to thin if needed.

Store in the fridge, in an airtight jar, for 1–2 days.

CASHEW CREAM 'CHEEZE'

120g [1 cup]	cashews
juice of $\frac{1}{2}$	lemon
1 tbsp	nutritional yeast flakes
$\frac{1}{2}$ tsp	garlic powder
$\frac{1}{2}$ tsp	salt

SERVES 2

Soak the cashews in 600ml [$2\frac{1}{2}$ cups] water for 4–5 hours, then drain and rinse well in fresh water.

Put the soaked cashews in a food processor with 50ml [$3\frac{1}{2}$ tbsp] water. Add the remaining ingredients and process until smooth.

Store in the fridge, in an airtight jar, for 1–2 days.

HEMP HEART 'PARMESAN'

1 tbsp	hemp hearts [shelled hemp seeds]
1 tbsp	raw almonds
1 tbsp	nutritional yeast flakes
$\frac{1}{4}$ tsp	garlic powder
pinch	salt, to taste

SERVES 1–2

Place all the ingredients in a large bowl and, using a stick blender, whizz until smooth.

Store in the fridge, in an airtight jar, for 1–2 days.

EDAMAME 'HUMMUS'

100g [3½ oz] | frozen edamame beans, thawed and cooked
juice of ½ | lemon
1 tbsp | light tahini
¼ tsp | garlic powder
pinch | salt, to taste

SERVES 1-2

Place all the ingredients in a high-speed blender and whizz until smooth.

Store in the fridge, in an airtight jar, for 1–2 days.

SNACKS

POMEGRANATE + CHIA

4 tbsp	chia seeds
$\frac{1}{3}$ **tsp**	lemon peel, finely grated
150ml [$\frac{2}{3}$ cup]	pomegranate + lemon juice [see page 34]
+	**TOPPINGS**
1 tbsp	shaved apple
1 tsp	fresh blueberries
5	fresh mint leaves

SERVES 2

Mix the chia seeds, lemon peel and juice together in a small jar. Leave to stand for 2–3 minutes, then stir again. Cover and chill in the fridge for at least 30 minutes to set.

Serve with all the toppings.

CHOCOLATE + COCONUT CHIA

3 tbsp	chia seeds
1 tbsp	raw cacao powder
pinch	vanilla powder
pinch	ground cinnamon
pinch	salt
150ml [$\frac{2}{3}$ cup]	coconut milk
1 tbsp	coconut nectar, to taste

+ TOPPINGS

1 tbsp	fresh raspberries
1 tsp	coconut flakes
1 tsp	cacao nibs

MAKES 1-2

Mix the chia seeds and other dry ingredients together in a small jar. Add the coconut milk and nectar and leave to stand for 2-3 minutes, then stir again. Chill in the fridge for at least 30 minutes to set.

Serve with all the toppings.

TIP: If you're using coconut milk from a can, make sure it's smooth and not lumpy. If the coconut milk has separated into cream and liquid, blend it first to combine them together again.

BLUEBERRY + VANILLA CHIA

3 tbsp	chia seeds
1 tbsp	blueberry powder or fresh blueberries
$\frac{1}{2}$ tsp	ground cardamom
pinch	vanilla powder
150ml [$\frac{2}{3}$ cup]	almond milk [see page 27]

+ TOPPINGS

1 tbsp	fresh blueberries or bilberries
1 tsp	coconut flakes
1 tsp	dried mulberries

SERVES 1-2

Mix the chia seeds, blueberry powder and spices together in a small jar. Add the almond milk and leave to stand for 2-3 minutes. Stir again and chill in the fridge for at least 30 minutes to set.

Serve with all the toppings.

FIG + CINNAMON PORRIDGE BARS

30g [¼ cup]	raw almonds, roughly chopped
50g [⅓ cup]	dried figs, roughly chopped
60g [¾ cup]	rolled oats
65g [½ cup]	sesame seeds
2 tbsp	chia seeds
3 tbsp	desiccated coconut
½ tbsp	ground cinnamon
1½ tbsp	coconut oil, melted
1 tsp	honey or maple syrup for a vegan option [optional]

MAKES 12 BARS

Mix the almonds, figs, oats, seeds, coconut and cinnamon together in a bowl.

In a jug, mix the sweetener [if using] and coconut oil with 100ml [7 tbsp] water [the water shouldn't be too cold otherwise the oil may turn solid again]. Stir the coconut oil mixture into the dry ingredients until combined. Place the 'dough' in an airtight rectangular container and spread it evenly on the base of the container, pressing it down with your fingers. Smooth the surface with a spoon, then cover with a lid and chill in the fridge for at least 2 hours.

Cut the solid 'dough' still in the container into 6 bars or 12 smaller bites with a knife, then invert the container to remove them. You can knock the bottom of the inverted box if the bars get stuck, as this won't break them. Enjoy as snacks or crumble the bars into pieces to eat on top of yogurt or chia porridge instead of muesli or granola.

Store in the fridge, in an airtight container, for up to 2 days.

SOUR CHERRY + VANILLA PORRIDGE BARS

30g [¼ cup]	raw almonds, roughly chopped
60g [¾ cup]	rolled oats
65g [½ cup]	sesame seeds
2 tbsp	chia seeds
50g [½ cup]	dried sour cherries or cranberries
3 tbsp	desiccated coconut
½ tbsp	vanilla powder
1½ tbsp	coconut oil, melted
1 tsp	honey or maple syrup for a vegan option [optional]

MAKES 12 BARS

Mix the almonds with all the other dry ingredients together in a bowl.

In a jug, mix the sweetener [if using] and coconut oil with 100ml [7 tbsp] water [the water shouldn't be too cold otherwise the oil may turn solid again]. Stir the coconut oil mixture into the dry ingredients until combined. Place the 'dough' in an airtight rectangular container and spread it evenly on the base of the container, pressing it down with your fingers. Smooth the surface with a spoon, then cover with a lid and chill in the fridge for at least 2 hours.

Cut the solid 'dough' in the container into 6 bars or 12 smaller bites with a knife, then invert the container to remove them. You can knock the bottom of the inverted box if the bars seem stuck, as this won't break them. Enjoy as snacks or crumble the bars into pieces to eat on top of yogurt or chia porridge instead of muesli or granola.

Store in the fridge, in an airtight container, for up to 2 days.

CHOCOLATE + MACA BLISS BALLS

1 tbsp	almond flour
3 tbsp	desiccated coconut, plus extra for coating
1 tbsp	raw cacao powder, plus extra for coating
1 tbsp	carob powder
1 tsp	maca powder
$\frac{1}{2}$ tsp	vanilla powder
pinch	salt
10	dates, pitted
1 tbsp	smooth almond or peanut butter
$\frac{1}{2}$ tbsp	lingonberry powder, for coating

MAKES 12 BALLS

Mix all the dry ingredients together in a bowl. Place all the ingredients in a high-speed blender or food processor and whizz until you have a sticky, smooth dough. Divide the dough into 12 even-sized pieces and roll into balls.

Spread the coconut, cacao and lingonberry powder for coating out on shallow plates. Roll the balls evenly in the cacao, coconut and lingonberry powder until they are coated all over. Refrigerate for at least an hour before serving.

The balls are best enjoyed cold.

GINGERBREAD BLISS BALLS

1 tsp	coconut oil
50ml [3½ tbsp]	ginger juice
15g [⅛ cup]	cashews, chopped
15g [scant ¼ cup]	almond flour
10g [⅛ cup]	desiccated coconut
½ tsp	ground cinnamon, plus extra for coating
½ tsp	ground cardamom
pinch	vanilla powder
10	dates, pitted

MAKES 12 BALLS

Melt the coconut oil in a heatproof bowl set over a pan of gently simmering water. Remove from the heat and stir in the ginger juice.

Mix all the dry ingredients together in a bowl. Place all the ingredients in a high-speed blender or food processor and whizz until you have a sticky, smooth dough. Divide the dough into 12 even-sized pieces and roll into balls.

Roll the balls in the extra cinnamon. Refrigerate for at least an hour before serving.

The balls are best enjoyed cold.

TAHINI + LIQUORICE BLISS BALLS

25g [$\frac{1}{4}$ cup]	almond flour
1 tbsp	blueberry powder
1 tsp	liquorice powder
250g [1$\frac{1}{2}$ cups]	soft pitted prunes [dried plums]
1 tbsp	black tahini [see page 138]
2 tbsp	black and white sesame seeds, for coating

MAKES 12 BALLS

Mix all the dry ingredients together in a bowl. Place all the ingredients in a high-speed blender or food processor and whizz until you have a sticky, smooth dough. Divide the dough into 12 even-sized pieces and roll into balls.

Spread the black and white sesame seeds out on separate, shallow plates and roll the balls in them until they are coated all over. Refrigerate for at least an hour before serving.

The balls are best enjoyed cold.

INDEX

ACKNOWLEDGEMENTS

MUM For always pushing and encouraging me to be the best version of myself and inspiring me to work hard towards turning my dreams into a reality no matter how big they were.

RICHARD For being the craziest and most creative [and best] business partner I could imagine and helping me cook everything for this book.

ANDREW Our third cookbook together [with more to come], I think this proves that we are a dream team when it comes to photography and styling. Thank you.

ROMILLY My fellow Aries. Upon meeting you, I knew immediately this book would turn out just how I wanted it to and even better. You're a very talented, creative and beautiful person and I couldn't have wished for a better editor.

NIKKI For making my vision of an art book meets cookbook come true and for pairing one-by-one my hand-drawn illustrations to the recipe images and making it all seem so easy and smooth.

L, L, L, A, M + J For being my best friends and soul sisters for over ten years and always volunteering for testing any new recipes.

Suzanne Sullivan Ceramics for hand-crafting some of the custom spoons for this book. **SunSpelt** for producing organic, Finnish quinoa that is perfect for porridge and **Arctic Power Berries** for making the Finnish berry magic available to the whole world in the form of freeze-dried berry powders.

And most of all, to the growing, like-minded community all over social media and in real life too, for continuously inspiring and encouraging me to create more and more plant-based goodness.

THIS BOOK IS FOR YOU.

ANNI KRAVI is a Helsinki-based recipe developer and food artist who has over 50K followers on Instagram @anniskk. She has developed an international following for her beautiful and meditative preparation of bowl food. She has been titled 'the queen of porridge' and this is her first book on the subject.